THE RAILWAY CARTOON BOOK

KEN AND KATE BAYNES

DAVID & CHARLES

Newton Abbot   London   North Pomfret (Vt)   Vancouver

ACKNOWLEDGEMENTS

This book could not have worked up a good head of steam without a great deal of enthusiastic stoking from individuals and institutions. Many have given us advice and have suggested new sources of laughter. We are particularly grateful to Mr E Wood and Mr S J Woodward of the Great Western Railway Museum; Peter Lawrence; George Ottley at the University of Leicester; Dr J A Coiley at the National Railway Museum; Mrs E Coles and Mr H Woolfe at the Science Museum Library.

Chris Ridley and Gerald Pates have had the difficult task of photographing much of the material. Even with so much mixed freight to contend with, they have done an excellent job. Jane Bingham and Pauline Riley have coped patiently with the secretarial work.

KEN AND KATE BAYNES
Whiteshill, April 1976

ISBN 0 7153 7354 4
Library of Congress Catalog Card
Number: 76 40617

© Ken and Kate Baynes 1976

Set in Aldine Roman and Printed in Great Britain by Biddles Limited, Guildford for David and Charles (Publishers) Limited Brunel House Newton Abbot Devon

Published in the United States of America by David and Charles Inc North Pomfret Vermont 05053 USA

Published in Canada by Douglas David and Charles Limited 1875 Welch Street North Vancouver BC

Book designed by Ken and Kate Baynes

Title page
Cartoon from Punch, 1857. From the Mansell Collection, London, Photographer Gerald Pates

The Imperial War Museum has kindly given permission for the reproduction of the detail of a wartime poster on the cover (see page 73)

Reading Between the Lines.

Cartoon *Reading Between the Lines* from the magazine
Scraps, 1887. Collection of Peter Lawrence.
Photographer Chris Ridley

Cartoon by George Cruickshank from the period of the Railway Mania. Mansell Collection, London. Photographed by Gerald Pates

Drawing illustrating the Song of the Railway Porter from *The Comic Bradshaw* by Angus B Reach, 1848. National Railway Museum, York

INTRODUCTION

The railways occupied a unique place in Nineteenth century life. They were a technological marvel and an everyday experience. As a result, they came to be second only to politics and the comedy of manners as a subject for cartoonists. It is impossible to open an issue of *Punch* from the last years of Victoria's reign without finding at least one joke about trains and it was the same wherever else humourists tried to raise a laugh. Cartoonists looked on railways with a wry but affectionate humour. It was an attitude that perfectly reflected the truth that they were a fascinating, imperfect but indispensible adjunct to the life and prosperity of the times.

By 1900 trains and stations had become completely domesticated : a stage set for encounters between variegated travellers who reflected every aspect of society. But this familiarity was something which only evolved over a period of time. To start with it was simply the phenomenon of railways that held the cartoonists' imagination. They did not like what they saw. Technical progress has always been regarded as a mixed blessing, particularly so by humourists who tend naturally to be conservatives with a small 'c'. Attack is, in any case, funnier than defence. They were forthright spokesmen for the opposition. Cartoonists lampooned the easy optimism of those who hailed the steam locomotive as 'the Con-

quering Hero'. They saw, instead, the 'Railway Dragon' and showed that by such adlepated enthusiasm supporters of railways were helping the iron road in its work of driving people mad, despoiling the countryside, upsetting the lower orders, fomenting sedition and were – quite certainly – flying in the face of the Creator.

The mixture of scepticism, wonder and optimism which characterised this early period of railway development is nicely caught by Paul Hawkins Fisher, the nineteenth century historian of our own local town of Stroud. The Great Western Railway was opened to this part of Gloucestershire in May 1845. Looking back on the event Fisher wrote that 'the huge iron horse with his eyes of fire, his breath of flame, and his long white mane of steam ... then came, to startle us from our propriety ... snorting, shrieking, roaring, and seeming to swallow the ground as it flashes through our beautiful valleys, at the speed of thirty miles an hour.' He went on 'We have thus acquired greater rapidity and perhaps greater safety, in travelling than formerly. But there are many who continue to regret the loss of their pleasant journeys on a well appointed coach, through the invigorating air and magnificent scenery of our picturesque neighbourhood.' No doubt distance lent charm to the rigours of travel by coach, but this sense of loss and disturbance was widespread and the cartoonists were unanimous in attacking those who had the temerity to startle people from their propriety. They had a field day but they didn't stop the conquering hero. More powerful forces — industry, profit, progress — were pushing it irresistably forwards.

During the railway mania the attitude of outrage reached new heights. When the bubble of railway speculation burst, and many small investors lost their savings, fierce vituperation was directed towards the boards of the luckless companies. At the centre of the storm was George Hudson, the railway king. His financial wizardry and unscrupulousness changed the transport map of nineteenth century Britain but his magic could not, in the end, stave off a disastrous crash. When it came, it involved the highest in the land.

The mania and the subsequent collapse of the market coincided with the end of the first phase of railway cartooning. As the companies established themselves as great institutions and travel by train became more and more a common experience, so we begin to see the emergence of the kind of jokes with which we are still familiar. In the chapter on First Class — Third Class we have tried to present a reasonably complete range of the possible encounters between incompatible fellow travellers. They remain as fresh and funny as ever because they can still be experienced. A shorthand of human characters brings them readily to mind:

Formidable old gentleman defeated by ghastly child
Gentility badgered by vulgarity
Non smoker fumigated by smoker
Fug lover ventilated by fresh air fiend

"AN OFFICER AND A GENTLEMAN!"

Volunteer Captain (bumptiously). "OFFICER'S TICKET!"
Considerate Clerk. "GOVER'MENT TARIFF'S HIGH ON THIS LINE, SIR. YOU'D BETTER GO AS A GENTLEMAN! CHEAPER!"
[*The Captain is shocked, loses his presence of mind, and takes advantage of the suggestion.*

Face from *The Comic Bradshaw* by Angus B Reach, 1848. National Railway Museum, York

Cartoon from *Punch*, 1868. Collection of Ken and Kate Baynes. Photographer Gerald Pates

"*All favourites again. First, Green Trees. Second, The Elms. Third,*
dead heat, Sans Souci and The Cedars."

Cartoon by David Langdon from *Lilliput*, 1947.
Collection of Ken and Kate Baynes. Photographer
Gerald Pates

Innocent young thing subjected to worldly wise attentions

And so on. The cartoonists depicted these timeless meetings in the setting of the Victorian world of social etiquette and attitude and they did it with a beautiful precision. Their drawings not only tell us what these travellers looked like and what kinds of clothes they wore, they tell us as well about what they believed and how they regarded one another. If it is the vituperative fantasy that is attractive in the early cartoons, here what holds attention is the realism and exactitude of the social observation that accompanies the joke. It is a precision of observation which cartoonists like Pont continued to provide between the two world wars and which Giles has triumphantly continued into the present. Through their eyes we can see how the travelling public has evolved over a period of a hundred and thirty years and we can observe the interesting fact that, when he is on a train, the Englishman — or woman — is very English indeed!

Just because the railway companies became respectable and accepted, it does not follow that criticism ceased. The cartoonists found a whole catalogue of shortcomings to present. Again they are familiar. Late running, incomprehensible timetables, arrogant officials, dirty compartments: all

these appear to be and to have been the universal accompaniments of rail travel. But by the height of the Victorian era a lot of the sting had gone out of even these justifiable complaints. When the railway dragon ceased to breath fire, it evidently became a pet. Incorrigibly naughty and mischievous perhaps, but clearly loved even in spite of its many shortcomings.

For some, railway travel became indispensible to their way of life. Without railways, the tidy, gentle, boring suburbs with their streets named after trees and flowers would not have come into existence. Without hundreds of eightfifteens leaving the Clyde Coast or Blackpool or Clapham or High Barnet, millions of clerks, secretaries, managing directors and shopkeepers would not have had the pleasure of their little gardens on Summer evenings or the harmless satisfaction of polite, bourgeois society.

But it would be hard to define their attitude to railways as 'affectionate'. They were too often late home for dinner to allow room for that emotion. And it is interesting that although cartoonists did attack railways for their shortcomings in providing for their most faithful and regular customers, they also have a wry vision of the commuter himself. Observing his daily dash to the station and the sardine can provided by generous railway managements

anxious to maximise profits, it is as if humourists can't help seeing the humour of the situation. Being men privileged to lead a different kind of life they evidently feel sardonic and superior. Look, they seem to be saying, you brought this whole ridiculous thing on yourself. Don't expect sympathy from us: move back to town as God intended.

The London commuter eventually achieved the status of a minor hero. In the guise of David Langdon's Billy Brown of London Town, he survived the rigours of essential travel between 1939 and 1945. A lovely drawing shows bowler-hatted Billy and his wife stepping onto an escalator at three minutes to three. She has a bandana round her hair and a gas mask case at her side. He admonishes her in verse:

'You see, my dear', said BILLY BROWN
'How transport services in town
Begin their main rush-hours by 4
(Much earlier than before the war)
And so, when shopping, it's my view
That you and other shoppers too
Should try to start for home by 3'
'I will, my dear,' said Mrs B.

And they did. And put up with bombs and the black-out and a railway service disjointed by the necessity of carrying unheard of quantities of war-time freight. Most trav-ellers appear to have understood the difficulties which the railways were facing and it is certainly possible to detect a strong revival of affection during these years. The cartoonists were fascinated by two apparently irreconcileable tendencies. On the one hand, British life appeared quite unaffected by the war. On the other, completely unheard of things happened. The continuity is beautifully caught in a famous cartoon by Pont. It shows the somnolent evening of a country pub: all is peace and tranquillity. The radio reports from abroad 'meanwhile, in Britain, the entire population, faced by the threat of invasion, has been flung into a state of complete panic ...' Panic indeed!

The character of the new events showed themselves in the air-raid shelters that the underground stations became every evening. Here complete strangers began to talk to one another as if they had known each other for years. The contrast with the legendary iciness and trappist-like silence of the normal travelling Englishman was complete.

Hitler did not manage to destroy the steam railway in Britain but Doctor Beeching did. This event was hardly funny but it did create a storehouse of nostalgia for the days that had vanished. People began to love railways for themselves. Some draughtsmen

The Spirit of 1943

Lion drawn by L D Luard for London Transport.
Imperial War Museum, London. Photographer Eileen
Tweedy

The portraits and diagrams show the impression made by second class seats at various distances from starting
From *The Comic Bradshaw* by Angus B Reach, 1848. National Railway Museum, York

always had this point of view. For them the railway was a starting point for a journey into fantasy. They attempted to create a world that was more railway-like than real railways. Or perhaps they tried to see the Platonic essential behind all railways. W Heath Robinson, for example, took the dotty details of organisational and constructional splendour and translated them into an absolutely convincing other world of technological fantasy. Emmett took the cranky quintessence of the privately owned country branch line and equipped it with engineering skills that might have best appealed to Titania in Midsummer Night's Dream. To us, these appear to be serious men. The insight they offer into railways links up again with the first railway dragons. Like the early cartoonists, Heath Robinson and Emett try to tell us what railways *really* mean.*

What we hope this introduction indicates is that cartoonists have found in railways a very varied source of inspiration. The aim of the book is to allow the reader to share in the joke : to see railways through the eyes of those who made fun out of them. At the same time, it provides a window onto the social life of the Victorians. In their attitudes to travelling and travellers, they tell us a great deal about themselves. This window on their lives provides such an intriguing view because of the excellence

of nineteenth century drawing. It is journalistic, realistic, witty and full of incidental detail. We think it will provide one of the main pleasures of this collection.

There is one awful danger in attempting to introduce a funny book. Hanging humour around with sociology and history can easily turn out to be bunk. We hope we haven't fallen into that trap because we do think that there is a serious aspect to what we are showing. But most of all, of course, the cartoons are now, as they were always meant to be, funny and entertaining. That's why we selected them. As an antidote to excessive seriousness we cannot do better than end by quoting from 'The Comic Bradshaw or Bubbles from the Boiler' a Victorian book of humourous pieces about trains:

(Enter a Virtuous Indignation and High Art Writer, who turns up his nose at the idea of a book designed only to amuse people, and proffers to the PUBLISHER a MS intended as a railway brochure, being an 'Analysis of Aristotle's Metaphysics,' with a 'Dissertation on Bacon's Novum Organum,' a 'Pathetic Appeal on the Game Laws,' an 'Analytical Disquisition into the Nature of Circumstantial Nonentities,' an Essay on the Character of Hamlet,' and a 'Comparative Estimate of Beethoven and Bach.' The PUBLISHER falls into strong convul-

*owing to copyright difficulties we regret that it proved impossible to include examples of Emett's work in this book

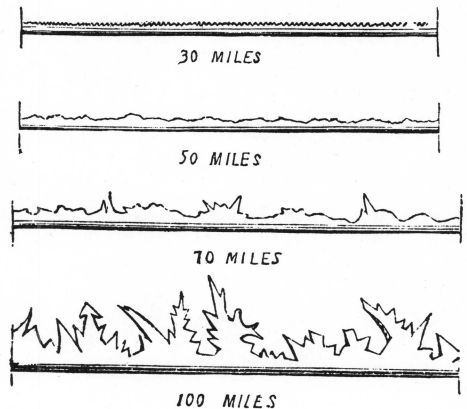

AT STARTING

sions, while the PUBLIC, AUTHOR and ARTIST, aided by the PORTERS, seize and bundle the High Art Gentleman into the Boiler, which sinks through a trap door, with blue fire, while the executioners of this act of justice soar upwards through the shaft singing,

    "We fly by night,
    When we've water and spirits".)

30 MILES

50 MILES

70 MILES

100 MILES

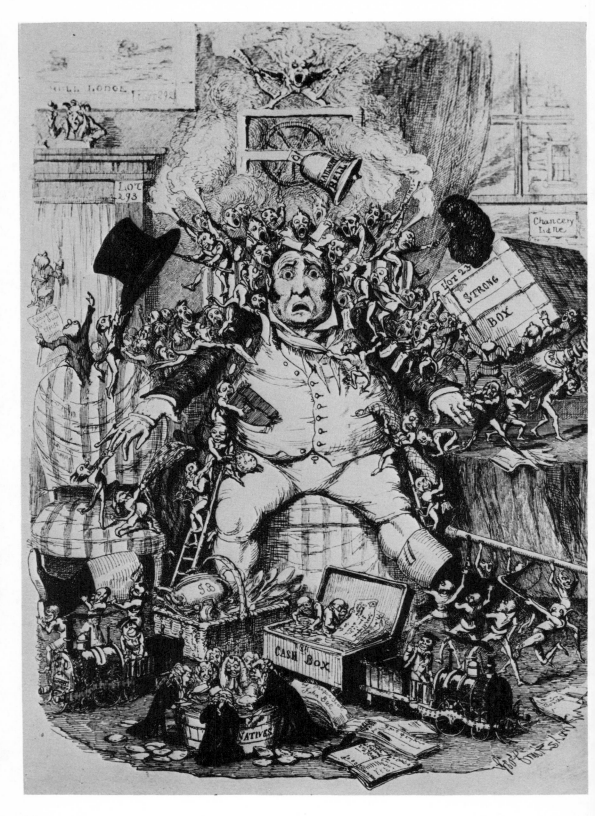

I COME TO EAT YOU UP

early years of the Railway dragon speculation and the railway mania

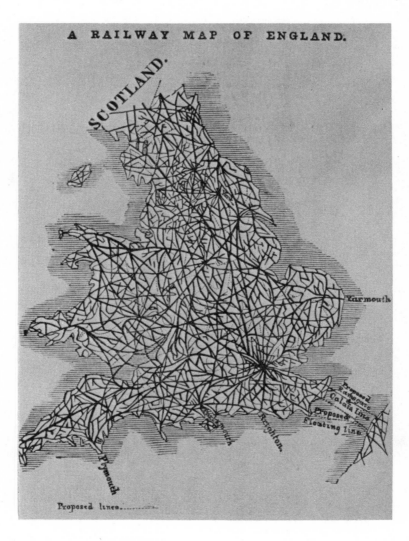

A RAILWAY MAP OF ENGLAND.

Mr John Bull in a Quandary by George Cruickshank.
Mansell Collection, London. Photographer Gerald Pates

Punch cartoon. Mansell Collection, London.
Photographer Gerald Pates

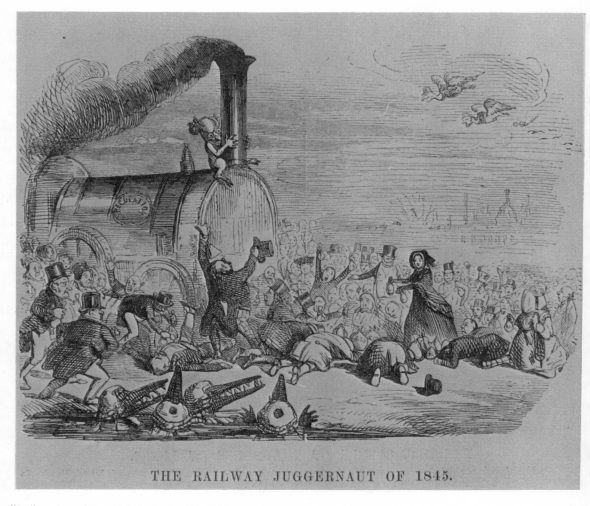

THE RAILWAY JUGGERNAUT OF 1845.

'Railway speculation had attained such a hold upon the
public mind that thousands rushed madly to their ruin'.
Mansell Collection, London. Punch, 1845. Photographer
Gerald Pates

The imaginary procession on the opening of the Railway
Parliament. 'The procession will open with *Punch* in
person, and his dog Toby in character, who will have at
his tail the Speaker, mounted on his engine of state,
drawn by a hundred of jet-black coals, and followed by
enthusiastic crowds....' Mansell Collection, London.
Punch, 1845. Photographer Gerald Pates

Printed linen handkerchief foretelling a future based on
steam power. John Johnson Collection, Bodleian Library,
Oxford. Circa 1850

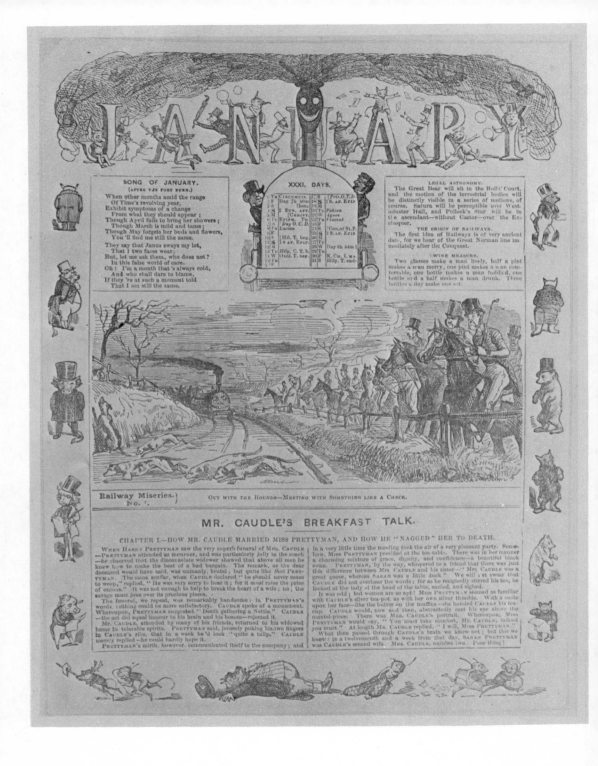

Two pages from *Punch's Almanack* for 1846, drawn by
J. Leech Mansell Collection, London.
Photographer Gerald Pates

JUNE

SONG OF JUNE.
(AFTER TENNYSON.)

The Bombyx—'tis a kind of moth—
Is active in the candle's glare,
And Nature spreads her greenest cloth,
To give the butterfly his fare.
The wings with little spots of grey,
Are open'd out at all their length,
As if the larvæ would display,
In such a month, their utmost strength.

I knew a miller in my youth,
He was too keen a man by half,
For when you thought he spoke the truth,
'Twas ten to one he gave you chaff.
And I have watched his fortunes sink,
Because his pride he would not prune;
But this has nought to do, I think,
With my poor song—the song of June.

OPERATIONS IN THE BOUDOIR.
(The London Season.)

Now cultivate carnation on cheeks with oriental bloom, and lilies with pearl powder. Gather up and dress carrots with infallible dye. Remove tan, freckles, pimples, with emollient lotion. Use SNOOKS's dentifrice, and take WALKER's pills for the complexion.

SUMMER RETREAT.

If you find London too hot to hold you, you cannot choose a better retreat than Boulogne for the purpose of taking it coolly.

DIRECTIONS TO RAILWAY TRAVELLERS.

If the seat opposite yours be vacant, rest your feet upon it, especially should your boots be muddy. The elbows make capital scrapers, and the back cushions answer very well for mats. As you pay first-class fare, you have a right to first-rate accommodation.

Railway Miseries. No. VI. SCENE.—*Grand Hotel, Bath Road.* TRAVELLER. "What! are there the horses?" OLD BOY. "E—es, sir; and I be the Po-ast Boy."

CHAP. VI.—SHOWING HOW CAUDLE BROUGHT HOME SOME "GOOD FELLOWS" TO SPEND THE EVENING, AND FOUND MRS. CAUDLE WITH SOME FEMALE FRIENDS AT TEA.

"I DIDN'T choose to say anything to you last night, Mrs. CAUDLE—no; you needn't tell me that; I know I didn't open my lips; don't I say so, woman?—I didn't speak, because indeed I was too tired. But I *do* think it hard that I can't leave the house for a few days, but I must find it swarming with petticoats when I come back. Your friends, as you call 'em! as if women could ever be friends! It's rather hard, with what I'm charged for housekeeping, that I must find the place like a fair. *You didn't expect me home till to-morrow?* Oh, no! Else I should have found you alone, and as mute as a mouse; and not a word would you have said to me about the pack of gossips you'd had about you!

"Now, Mrs. CAUDLE, for the future just remember one thing. Never think to expect me; for you shall never know the exact time when I shall come home. No; I shall always take you by surprise; as every man who'd know what his wife's about should do.

"Well, I think I may guess now where the housekeeping money goes to! Now, I can account for the grocer's bills—and I can't tell what their bills beside—when I see the people you have to eat tea up. And then when I bring home a few friends that I find aboard the steam-boat—good fellows, I know, every one of 'em; though I never saw 'em before—when I come home, I find my house full of silks and satins—a mountain of bonnets on my bed—and nothing fit for Christians to sit down to. And after such conduct you'll expect me to keep my temper? Yes; you'll open your eyes and affect to stare at me, if I only swear the smallest in the world—when, if you'd married some men, Mrs. CAUDLE, the house wouldn't have held you! Now, I should like to know what my friends thought of me last night—what they thought of you? Why, of course, they looked upon me as a fool, for putting up with your conduct as quietly as I did—whilst for you, but—I'll respect your feelings—I won't say what they must have thought of you.

"For an hour and a half, at least, did we wait for supper—if supper, indeed, you could call it; for I blushed at everything upon the table. An hour and a half. *There was nothing in the house; everything was to be got?* Why, that's what I complain of, woman. That's the very fault. I bring home a few friends to supper, and there's nothing in the house. But I come home, and I find you with I don't know what cotton-box acquaintances, and the house smelling of toast and tea-cake enough to ruin one.

"Now, Mrs. CAUDLE, if we wish to continue happy together, understand that I won't have it. If I can't give a little supper to friends at my own home, I'd better give up housekeeping altogether.

"Where's my hat and gloves? I dine out to-day."

Two pages from *Punch's Almanack* for 1846, drawn by
J. Leech. The November one shows someone who had
invested in railway shares and gone bankrupt, keeping
the bailiffs out. Mansell Collection, London.
Photographer Gerald Pates

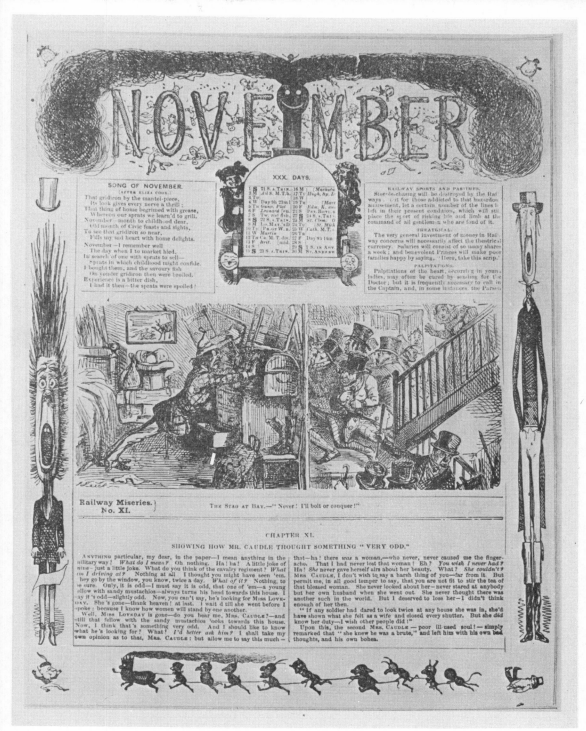

NOVEMBER

SONG OF NOVEMBER.
(AFTER ELIZA COOK.)

That gridiron by the mantel-piece,
Its look gives every nerve a thrill;
That thing of home begrimed with grease,
Whereon our sprats we learn'd to grill.
November—month to childhood dear,
thl month of Civic feasts and sights,
To see that gridiron so near,
Fills my sad heart with home delights.
November—I remember well
The day when I to market hied,
In search of one with sprats to sell—
"sprats in which childhood might confide.
I bought them, and the savoury fish
On yonder gridiron then were broiled,
Experience is a bitter dish,
I had it then—the sprats were spoiled!

XXX. DAYS.

RAILWAY SPORTS AND PASTIMES.
Steeple-chasing will be destroyed by the Railways. But for those addicted to that hazardous amusement, let a certain number of the lines be left in their present condition, which will still place the sport of risking life and limb at the command of all gentlemen who are fond of it.

THEATRICAL.
The very general investment of money in Railway concerns will necessarily affect the theatrical currency. Salaries will consist of so many shares a week; and benevolent Princes will make poor families happy by saying, "Here, take this scrip."

PALPITATIONS.
Palpitations of the heart, occurring in young ladies, may often be cured by sending for the Doctor; but it is frequently necessary to call in the Captain, and, in some instances, the Parson.

Railway Miseries. No. XI.

THE STAG AT BAY.—"Never! I'll bolt or conquer!"

CHAPTER XI.
SHOWING HOW MR. CAUDLE THOUGHT SOMETHING "VERY ODD."

ANYTHING particular, my dear, in the paper—I mean anything in the military way? What do I mean? Oh nothing. Ha! ha! A little joke of nine—just a little joke. What do you think of the cavalry regiment? What am I driving at? Nothing at all. I thought you might have seen 'em. hey go by the window, you know, twice a day. What of it? Nothing, to be sure. Only, it is odd—I must say it is odd, that one of 'em—a young fellow with sandy moustachios—always turns his head towards this house. I say it's odd—slightly odd. Now, you can't say, he's looking for Miss Lovejoy. She's gone—thank heaven! at last. I wait'd till she went before I spoke; because I know how women will stand by one another.

Well, Miss Lovejoy is gone—do you hear me, Mrs. Caudle?—and still that fellow with the sandy mustachios 'ooks towards this house. Now, I think that's something very odd. And I should like to know what he's looking for. What? I'd better ask him? I shall take my own opinion as to that, Mrs. Caudle: but allow me to say this much—

that—ha! there was a woman,—who never, never caused me the finger-ache. That I had never lost that woman! Eh? You wish I never had? Ha! She never gave herself airs about her beauty. What? She couldn't? Mrs. Caudle, I don't wish to say a harsh thing of you—far from it. But permit me, in all good temper to say, that you are not fit to stir the tea of that blessed woman. She never looked about her—never stared at anybody but her own husband when she went out. She never thought there was another such in the world. But I deserved to lose her—I didn't think enough of her then.

"If any soldier had dared to look twice at any house she was in, she'd have shown what she felt as a wife and closed every shutter. But she did know her duty—I wish other people did!"

Upon this, the second Mrs. Caudle—poor ill-used soul!—simply remarked that "she knew he was a brute," and left him with his own bad thoughts, and his own bohea.

LORD BROUGHAM'S RAILWAY NIGHTMARE.

Cartoon from *Punch* published during the Railway Mania
of 1849. Drawn by J. Leech. Mansell Collection, London,
photographer Gerald Pates

'The contemplated procession on the opening of the
Railway Parliament.... a series of frescoes by *Punch's*
artist....' Mansell Collection, London, 1845.
Photographer Gerald Pates

*Manners & Cuftoms of ye Englyfhe Drawn from ye Quick
By Richard Doyle* (sic). Book published in 1876, in the
collection of Ken and Kate Baynes. The illustration
shows a meeting of railway shareholders during the
Railway Mania of 1849

Cartoon from *Punch,* 1849. The Mansell Collection,
London

KING HUD

From a book in the North Yorkshire County Library
about the railway speculator George Hudson called
*How He Reigned and How He Mizzled, A Railway
Raillery.* *York ! You're Wanted !* Alfred Crowquill 1849.
Photographer Jim Kershaw

He squeezes the hand of Aristocracy(?)

He shows the Queen how to manage a Train.

24

S LEVEE.

He pretends to explain all for a Bob!!??

An Iron Duke goes the (Chemin de Fer)

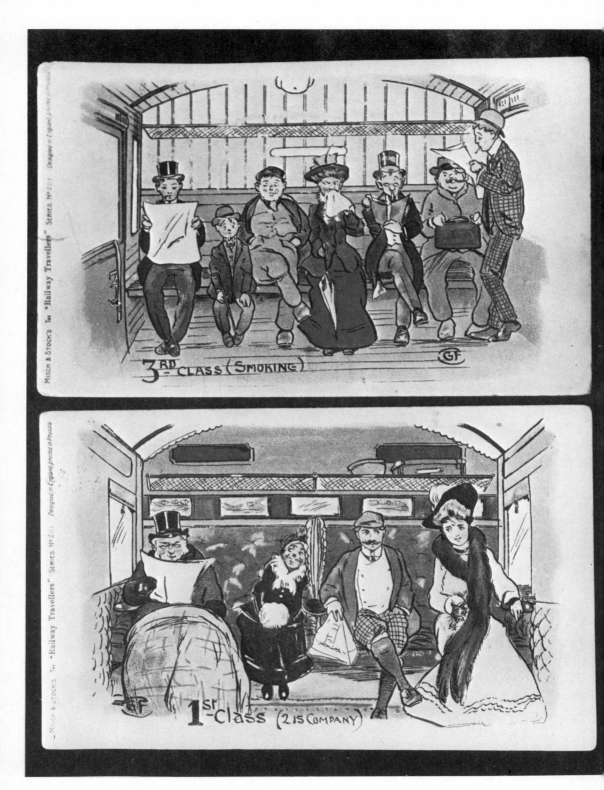

Two postcards from the collection of Peter Lawrence, photographed by Chris Ridley

'Love Me, Love my Dog' Punch, 1866. From collection of Ken and Kate Baynes. Photographer Gerald Pates

FIRST CLASS
THIRD CLASS

social attitudes and fellow travellers

"LOVE ME, LOVE MY DOG!"

Old Lady. "MARY, DEAR, WOULD YOU MIND CHANGING SEATS WITH POOR FLUFF? HE LIKES HAVING THE AIR IN HIS FACE!"

THE BUBBLES BLOWN.

Flight the Second.

THE FIRST-CLASS PASSENGER.

The first-class passenger 'keeps himself to himself, and seldom speaks except to the guard.'

The second-class passenger 'Is always anxious to tell you though he travels 'second', there is really no difference between that and the third-class that he could ever see' From *The Comic Bradshaw* by Angus B Reach, 1848. National Railway Museum, York

The third-class passenger regaling himself on 'half a stale quartern loaf and a ponderous lump of double Gloucester.' From *The Comic Bradshaw* by Angus B Reach, 1848. National Railway Museum, York

Lord Knaresborough, Chairman of the North Eastern
Railway. A lithograph by Spy published in *Vanity Fair*
in 1887. National Railway Museum, York

Three postcards from the collection of Peter Lawrence, photographed by Chris Ridley

Cover of a magazine from the collection of Peter Lawrence, dated 1901

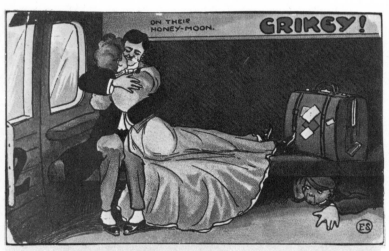

THIS PAPER IS A RAILWAY ACCIDENT LIFE POLICY FOR £150.

ally Sloper's Half Holiday

FOUNDED AND CONDUCTED BY GILBERT DALZIEL
SATURDAY, JUNE 15, 1901.

Vol. XVIII.—No. 894.

ONE PENNY

OFF FOR THEIR ANNUAL.

The "Morning Post" says: "Among the nobility and gentry leaving town for the seaside, special mention must be made of MR. SLOPER and his brilliant and beautiful family, who attracted considerable attention by their dignified and courtly behaviour en route. MR. SLOPER (known as Beau Sloper, also known as Bow Street Sloper), with that inbred chivalry so characteristic of his race, endeavoured to render himself agreeable to a charming fellow passenger, but Mrs. Sloper, who acted as caterer, nipped the proceedings in the bud by exclaiming, 'Take your eyes off that, and fix 'em on me, the grub, and our hoffsprings.'"

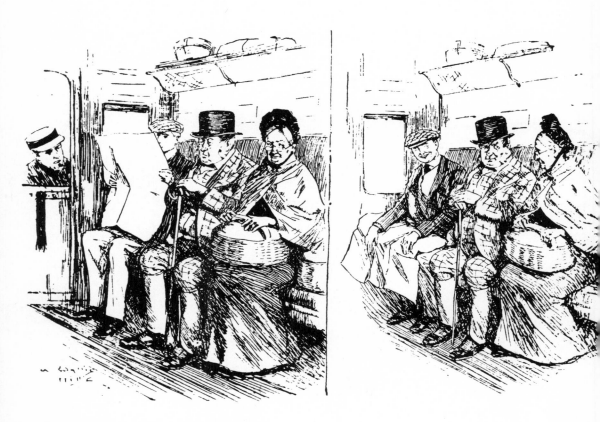

PORTER (at junction where all change for Glasgow,
Perth, and Paisley): Are any of you here for Perth,
Paisley, or Glasgow ?
Train moves off.
OLD LADY: I was for Glasgow myself, but I wasna
going to tell you speiring body.

From *The Wonder Book of Railways,* given as a Christmas
present to Kate Baynes's uncle in 1911. Photographer
Gerald Pates. Ward Lock and Co Ltd

CAUTION LARGE.

Volunteer (to Old Lady, who is calling the Guard, and making a great fuss about "the loaded Gun"). "I ASSURE YOU IT'S ALL RIGHT, MUM. I FIRED IT OFF BEFORE I LEFT THE CAMP."

Old Lady. "OH, BUT ONE CAN'T BE TOO CAREFUL. THERE MAY BE SOME OF IT LEFT IN !!"

From *Punch,* 1868. Collection of Ken and Kate Baynes.
Photographer Gerald Pates

CONDESCENDING.

Master Tom (going back to School, to Fellow Passenger). "IF YOU'D LIKE TO SMOKE, YOU KNOW, GOV'NOUR, DON'T YOU MIND ME, I RATHER LIKE IT!"

Mother. 'You don't mind for a few minutes, Sir ?
Yer see, 'is Father 'asn't got a beard.'

SHOWING WHAT A WONDERFUL IMPROVEMENT THE HOLES IN THE RAILWAY CARRIAGES ARE, PARTICULARLY DURING THE HOLIDAYS.

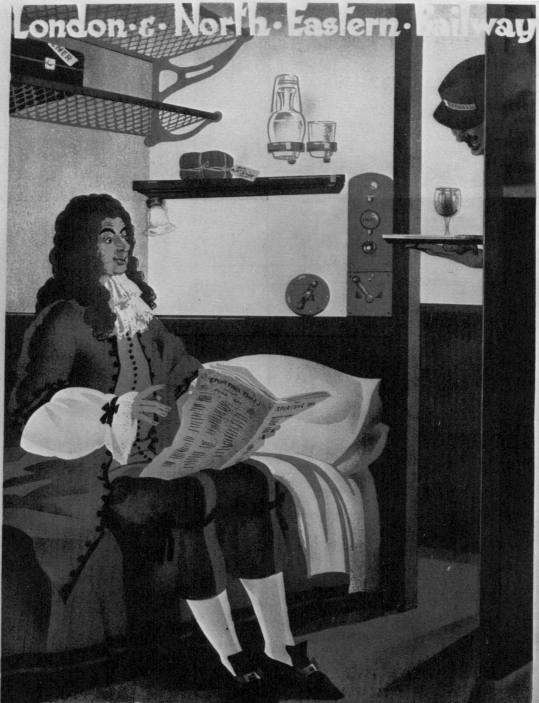

Poster for the London and North Eastern Railway by
Austin Cooper. National Railway Museum, York

'Put it In The Van Sir?' by Lawson Wood. National
Railway Museum, York

39

Policeman. "YOU MUST TAKE YOUR PLACE AT THE END OF THE QUEUE, MADAM, AND WAIT YOUR TURN."
Traveller. "BUT, GOOD *GRACIOUS*, MAN! I'VE GOT TO CATCH A TRAIN."

Cartoon drawn for *Punch* in 1919 by A Wallis Mills,
Collection of Ken and Kate Baynes. Photographer Gerald
Pates

Details from a cartoon in *Punch*, 1886. Titled *Rather
'Cute* it shows a clash between a sharp passenger and a
not-so-sharp booking clerk. There is an exchange about
change. At the denouement the passenger announces:
'Well, it's of no consequence to me; but you gave me
Half-a-Sovereign too Much! Ta-Ta!'

Traveller. "ONE V'GINIA WATER." Booking Clerk. "SINGLE?"
Traveller. "NO, DOUBLE: AND PUT SOME ICE IN IT."

From *Punch,* 1919. Collection of Ken and Kate Baynes.
Photographer Gerald Pates

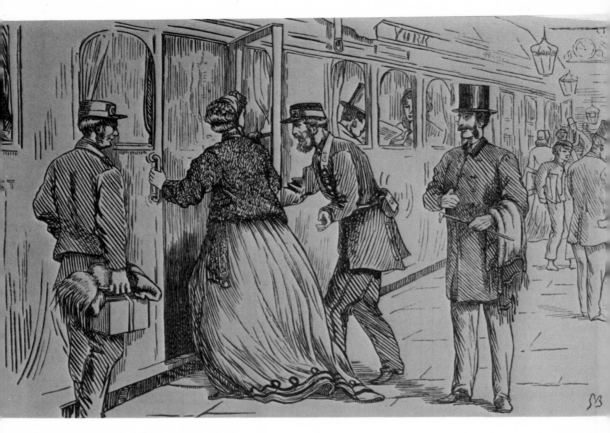

Two may be company, Three are none. Emily and Fred
have arranged to take care of each other, part of the way.
Polite guard cuts in (supposing E. unprotected). 'There's a
lady in the next carriage, Miss.' *(E. doesn't seem to see it).*

From *Punch,* 1866. Collection of Ken and Kate Baynes.
Photographer Gerald Pates

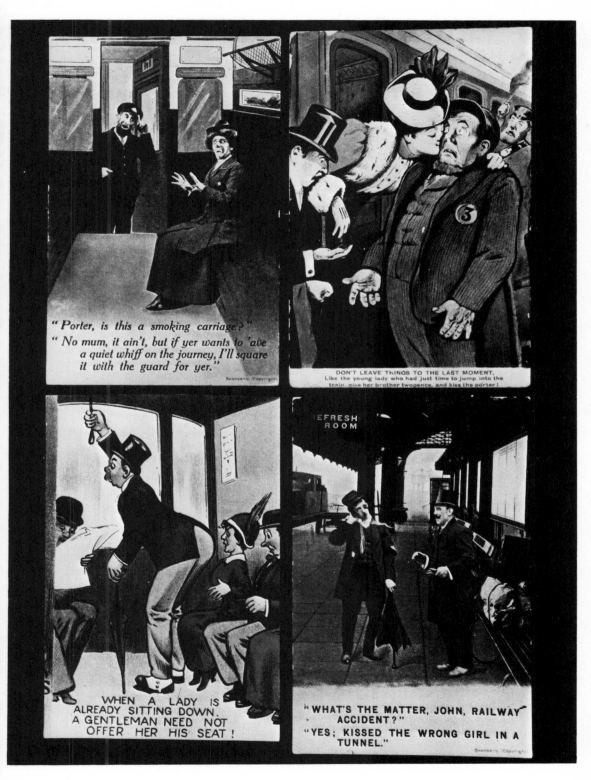

Five postcards from Peter Lawrence's collection,
photographed by Chris Ridley

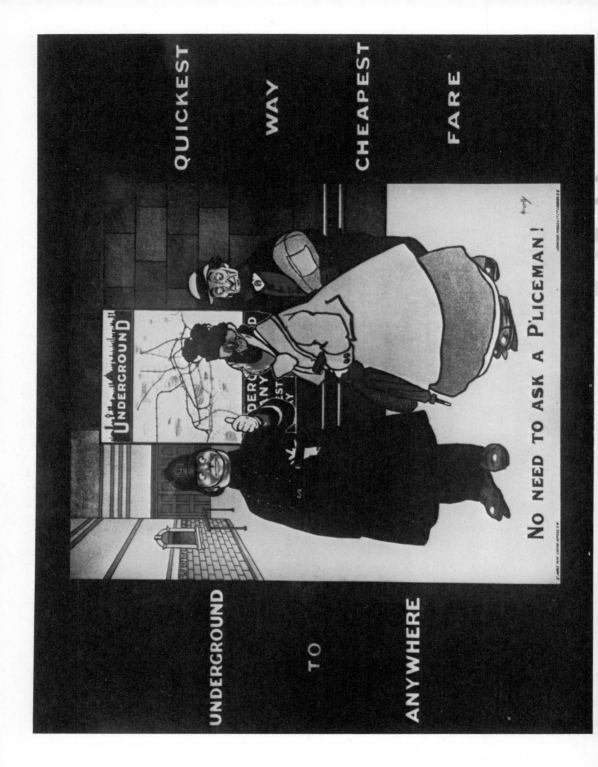

44

No need to ask a P'liceman ! by John Hassell . From a
London Transport poster of 1908

'Bean't that marvellous, Agnes ? Plumb in the 'ole every
time.' *Punch,* 1919. Collection of Ken and Kate Baynes

Flowers of speech

Cartoon from *The Pop Annual* published by The Daily
Graphic and Sunday Graphic Ltd. Collection of Ken and
Kate Baynes. Photographer Gerald Pates

Cartoon by Giles from the Daily Express, 1968. 'Taint
fair. I was looking forward to smashing up two special
football trains this week'
London Express News and Feature Services

SPADES ARE TRUMPS.

NAVVY (to Ab—rd—n).— "NOW, OLD STICK-IN-THE-MUD, LET *ME* TRY IF I CAN GET YOU OUT OF THE MESS.'

. The terrible condition of the Army in the Crimea being greatly increased for want of roads, a corps of navvies was sent out.—1855.

Poster for London Transport by Eric H Kennington, 1944.
Imperial War Museum, London. Photographer Eileen
Tweedy

Cartoon from *Punch*, 1855

Thank you, Mrs. Porter,
  For a good job stoutly done:
Your voice is clear, and the Hun can hear
  When you cry "South Kensington!"

The world must hurry homeward,
  The soldier on his way,
And the wheels whizz round on the Underground
  At the voice of the girls in grey.

And though the skies are noisy
  How calm the voices are—
"Upminster train!   That man again!
  Pass further down the car!"

                         A. P. Herbert

MANAGER'S
OFFICE
PRIVATE

A SUGGESTION.

A New Game, in Humble Imitation of Kriegspiel, to Enable Railway Directors to Conduct their Experiments without Loss of Life; and to Teach them their Business generally.

A cartoon about railway mismanagement from *Fun*, 1872. This was a working class version of *Punch* which frequently supported agitation for better conditions and better pay on the railways. Collection of Peter Lawrence. Photographer Chris Ridley

Cartoon about congestion on holiday trains in the period immediately following the first world war. *Punch*, 1919. Collection Ken and Kate Baynes. Photographer Gerald Pates

RAILWAY TIME
AND TRIALS

**a catalogue of shortcomings and disasters
scenes from commuting life
the railways in wartime**

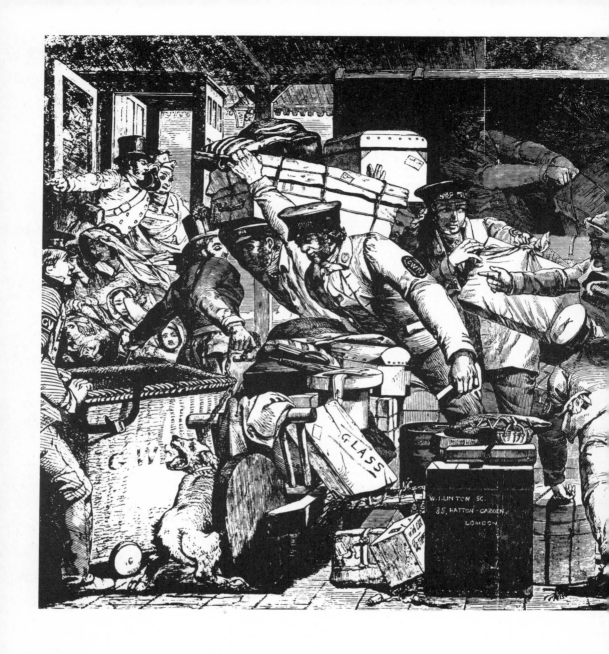

The Break of Gauge at Gloucester. Passengers and
Luggage being shifted from the broad gauge to the
narrow gauge carriages. G W R Museum, Swindon,
Photographers Cavill and Davison

Detail from a Giles cartoon published in the *Daily
Express* during the 1960 rail-strike. Collection of John
Frost. Photographer Gerald Pates

The Gentleman who was locked up, because he had lost his Ticket.

A family applying Wray's Aromatic Spice Plaster, preparatory to undertaking a journey by the Railroad.

Two drawings from a series of ten at the G W R Museum, Swindon. Photographers Cavill and Davison

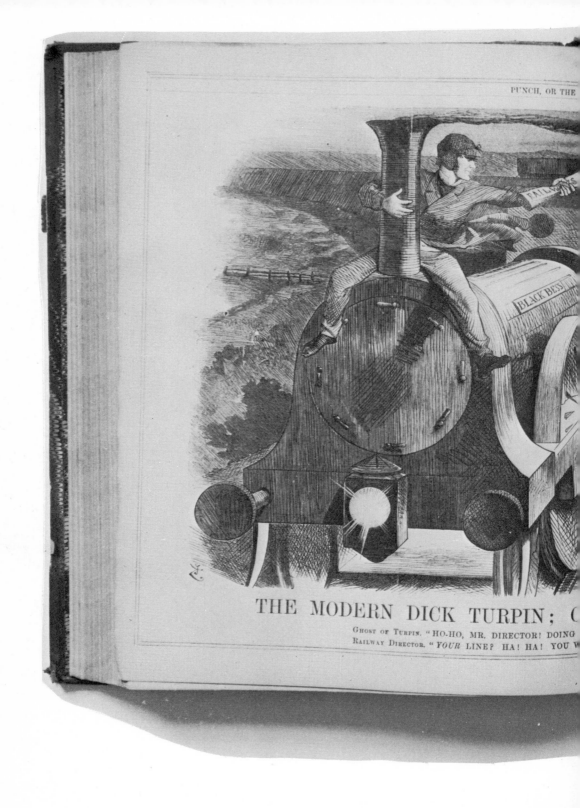

THE MODERN DICK TURPIN;

GHOST OF TURPIN. "HO-HO, MR. DIRECTOR! DOING

RAILWAY DIRECTOR. "*YOUR* LINE? HA! HA! YOU W

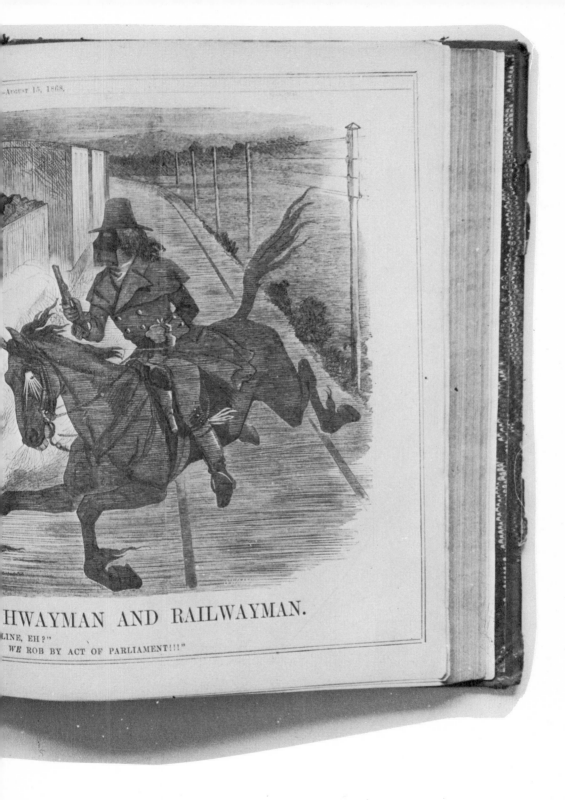

HWAYMAN AND RAILWAYMAN.

LINE, EH?"
WE ROB BY ACT OF PARLIAMENT!!!"

Cartoon from *Punch*, 1868. Collection Ken and Kate
Baynes. Photographer Gerald Pates

Cartoon from *Punch*, 1852. Railway Amalgamation —
A pleasant state of things.

PASSENGER.—"What's the matter, Guard?"
GUARD *(with presence of mind.)*—"Oh, nothing
particular, Sir. We've only run into an Excursion Train!"

PASSENGER.—"But, Good Gracious! there's a Train just
behind us, isn't there?"
GUARD.—"Yes, Sir! But a boy has gone down the line
with a signal; and it's very likely they'll see it!"

Cartoon from *Punch*, 1852. Railway Undertaking
TOUTER.—"Going by this Train, Sir?"
PASSENGER.—"'M? Eh? Yes."
TOUTER.—"Allow me, then, to give you one of my
Cards, Sir."

59

THE RAILWAY JUGGERNAUT!

From a magazine called *Fun,* read by the working
classes and now quite rare because it was usually thrown
away after being read. 1872. Collection of Peter
Lawrence, photographed by Chris Ridley

THE HOHENZOLLERN TOUCH.

PRESIDENT OF THE N.U.R. (*recalling his own Plymouth speech*). "WE WANT THE EARTH AND ALL THAT THEREIN IS!"

MR. J. H. THOMAS. "IS THAT 'DEFINITIVE,' CRAMP? THAT'S WHAT THE KAISER SAID IN 1914. I SHOULD LEAVE A LITTLE BIT FOR THE COMMUNITY."

Anti trades union cartoon from *Punch*, 1919. Collection of Ken and Kate Baynes. Photographer Gerald Pates

BEECHING SPECIAL

" YES, BUT WHERE'S THE TRAIN GOING, GUARD ? "

Newspaper cartoon by Dick German published in the
South Wales News in 1923. From *Brunel and After, The
Romance of the Great Western Railway* by Archibald
Williams. National Railway Museum, York

Cartoon by David Low published in the *Manchester
Guardian* in 1963. London Express News and Feature
Services

Cartoon by George Strube from the *Daily Express*, 1946.
London Express News and Feature Services

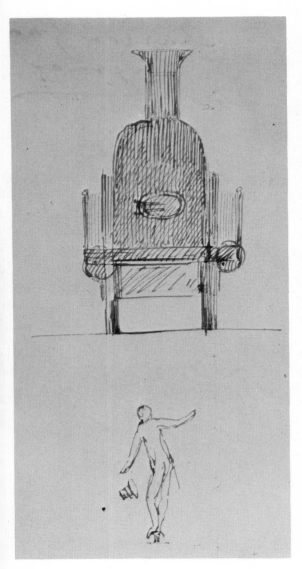

Cartoon by Charles Grave from *Punch,* 1919, captioned
Enthusiast: "I tell you the development of
the locomotive is simply wonderful. Why, that engine-
driver weighs more than the old 'Rocket' "

A broad-gauge engine driver fraternising with a narrow-
gauge engine driver after an amicable settlement of the
dispute, by W Heath Robinson from *Railway Ribaldry*
published by Ian Allan

Pen and ink sketches entitled broad and narrow gauge,
c. 1840. G W R Museum, Swindon. Photographers
Cavill and Davison

OUR RAILWAY AT CHRISTMAS.

Time—Dusk.

Season-Ticket Holder. "What o'clock was that struck? Five? Come on, then. If we make haste, we may be in time for the 2·15!"

From *Punch*, 1919. Photographed by Gerald Pates

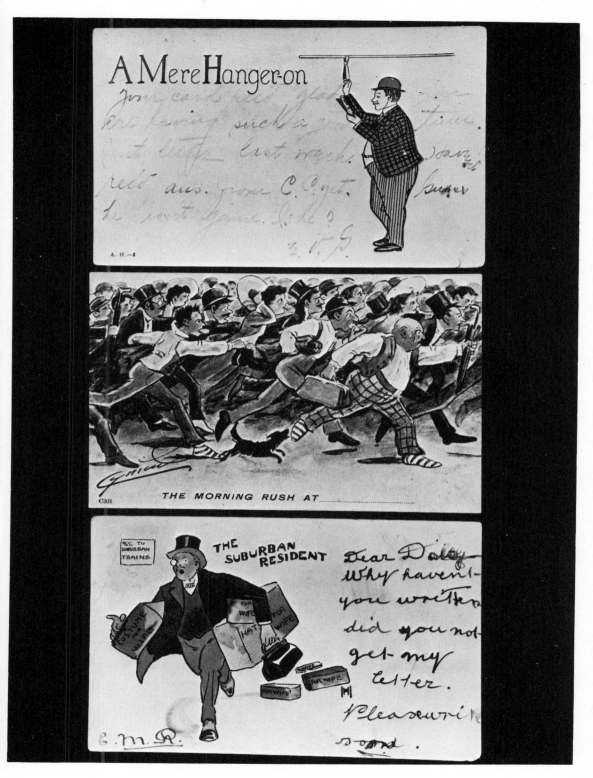

Postcards from the Peter Lawrence collection.
Photographer Chris Ridley

Cartoon from *Punch*. Collection of Ken and Kate Baynes.
H. M. Bateman, 1919. Photographer Gerald Pates

'The more we are together, the more uncomfortable we'll be. *PLEASE* PASS ALONG THE PLATFORM.' Poster by Fougasse for London Transport

Bristow on the underground, drawn for the *Evening Standard* by Frank Dickens. It was used by London Transport as a Christmas card

THE EXCURSIONIST

Tripper Wilhelm: "First Class to Paris.
Clerk: "Line blocked."
Wilhelm: "Then make it Warsaw."
Clerk: "Line blocked."
Wilhelm: "Well, what about Calais?"
Clerk: "Line blocked."
Wilhelm: "Hang it! I *must* go *somewhere!* I promised my people I would."

Two drawings from *Mr Punch's History of the Great War*,
published in 1919. Right: by F. W. Illingworth, 1914
Collection of Ken and Kate Baynes. Photographer Gerald Pates

Cartoon by Fougasse titled *The Shelter Trench* for *Punch*
from *I couldn't Help laughing.* Collection of Ken and
Kate Baynes. Photographer Gerald Pates

PORTER: "Do I know if the Rooshuns has really come to England? Well, sir, if this don't prove it, I don't know what do. A train went through here full, and when it came back I knowed there'd been Rooshuns in it; 'cause the cushions and floors was covered with snow."

Fourth and following hours

"Well, Mrs. Evans—is it?"

Wartime cartoon by Giles from *Laughs on the Home Front*, 1943. Collection of John Frost. Photographer Gerald Pates

HAVE YOUR
TICKETS READY
PLEASE

BRITISH RAILWAYS
G.W.R. L.M.S. L.N.E.R. S.R.
LONDON TRANSPORT

Wartime poster by Reginald Mayes. Imperial War
Museum. Photographer Eileen Tweedy

Billy's Bulletin

in the black-out tonight wear something white

No. ABB 1234　　　THIS YEAR, NEXT YEAR　　　A CRUSADE FOR WISER TRAVEL　　　PRICELESS

All the Browns (and Brownes) Agree—
LOOK OUT IN THE BLACK-OUT IS THE BEST POLICY

WHEN Billy Brown goes out at night he wears or carries something white. When Mrs. Brown is in the black-out she likes to wear her old white mack out.

And Sally Brown straps round her shoulder a natty plain white knick-knack holder.

before he crosses, if it's free; remembering when lights are dim that cars he sees may not see him.

The safest travelling in town is not too good for Billy Brown. He's much too sensible and knowing to jump down off a bus that's going, especially in black-out hours, or when the kerb is wet with showers. On these occasions Billy B. goes by the slogan 'Wait and See.'

. . so they may be seen at night

The reason why they wear this white is so they may be seen at night.

Down below the station's bright, but here outside it's black as night. Billy Brown will wait a bit and let his eyes grow used to it. Then he'll scan the road and see,

His slogan: Wait and See.

PATTERN SHOPPER

'YOU see, my dear,' said Billy Brown, 'how transport services in town begin their main rush-hours by 4 (much earlier than before the war). And so, when shopping it's my view that you, and other shoppers too, should try to start for home by 3.' 'I will, my dear', said Mrs. B.

*For copper rides, says Billy Brown,
I never tender half-a-crown:
The right amount saves much delay
And speeds the tram upon its way*

No Jam

NOT for our hero, anyhow. Not the sort of jam that spills out of a bottle-neck of overflowing traffic. But read on.

Billy finds it quite a strain to get himself inside a train: with such a squash around the door there's hardly room for any more. But down the car there's heaps of space and everyone could find a place. 'So let's all move along', says Billy: *'to crowd the entrance up is silly.'*

┌ Today's ┐ GOOD └ Deed ┘

WHEN you travel to and fro, on a line you really know, remember those who aren't so sure and haven't been that way before. Do your good deed for the day — *tell them the stations on the way.*

Many or few, it's
BETTER TO QUEUE

BILLY'S standing in a queue, as we all must sometimes do. Queueing in these days of rush means **you don't have any crush**, and the seconds saved will lend extra wings to journey's end. But, says Billy, see you choose the proper one of several queues!

WHAT'S IN A NAME?

THE answer is Everything—if you use it to good purpose, as Billy Brown does.

QUIZ CORNER

Says Billy Brown, 'It seems to me that things get lost quite needlessly. Because they bear no name inside they cannot be identified. *My name and address are found on everything I take around,* and so I'm very pleased to see you think it wise to copy me.'

*Billy Brown has had a rise in bus men's estimation
Since he paid the fare exact and named his destination*

Billy Brown's Own Highway Code—

He flags his bus with something white

for black-outs is 'Stay off the Road'. He'll never step out and begin to meet a bus that's pulling in. He doesn't wave his torch at night, but 'flags' his bus with something white. He never jostles in a queue, but waits and takes his turn— **Do you?**

That's the Stuff (*It may Save YOUR LIFE*)

IN the train a fellow sits and pulls the window-net to bits, because the view is somewhat dim, a fact which seems to worry him.

As Billy cannot bear the sight, he says 'My man, that is not right. **I trust you'll pardon my correction: That stuff is there for your protection.'**

THE WORLD'S MOST EXEMPLARY PASSENGER

When travelling on the Underground, you must have noticed, I'll be bound, little notes of friendly warning which one looks at every morning, referring to a Billy Brown, a citizen of London Town—a bloke who always does things right, a chap whose torch is not too bright, who scans his black-out every night, won't drive a car if he gets tight.

Now Billy, I have heard it said, would shake a disapproving head at those who never can refrain from scratching at the window pane. A glance would say, in their direction, 'This is here for your protection.' Of netted glass we see about the name is true, without a doubt. A time may come amidst the strife, when covered windows save a life.

Let us, then, not be forgetting of this, our duty to the netting.

Printed by Waterlow & Sons Limited, London, E.C.2, and published by London Transport at the Sign of the ⊖ 55 Broadway, London, S.W.1.　742—1700-C—2700.

LONDON TRANSPORT

Face the driver ● ─ ● ─
Face the driver ─ ● ─ ●

Do you use the BB Sign?

Hail your bus or tram in the correct way.

Face the driver, raise you hand—
You'll find that he will understand

STOP PRESS

'No Smoking' Rule Breach Significant Incident

At Bow Street Police Court today Billy Brown was commended by magistrate for frustrating attempt by passenger on Underground to smoke in car labelled 'No Smoking.'

Broadsheet published by London Transport during the Second World War. Drawings by David Langdon

74

'You see, my dear', said BILLY BROWN,
'How transport services in town
Begin their main rush-hours by 4
(Much earlier than before the war).
And so, when shopping, it's my view
That you and other shoppers too
Should try to start for home by 3'.
'I will, my dear', said Mrs. B.

Propaganda to persuade the public to travel outside peak
hours by London Transport. Drawings by David Langdon.
Second World War

PLEASE STAND ON THE RIGHT
OF THE ESCALATOR

Poster by Fougasse for London Transport. Second
World War

" *Yes, I pulled the cord. The wheels kept saying : ' Is your journey really necessary ? Is your journey really necessary ? Is your journey really necessary . . . ?' I just couldn't stand it any longer.*"

War time cartoon by David Langdon from *Punch*.
Photographer Gerald Pates

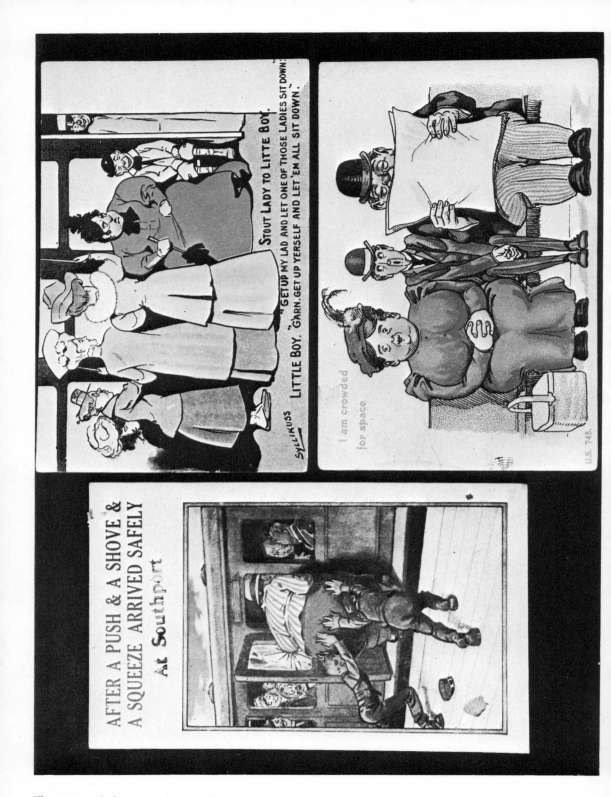

Three postcards from the collection of Peter Lawrence.
Photographer Chris Ridley

78

TRAVELLING BY WEIGHT.

[It is rumoured that one of the first steps to be taken by Sir ERIC GEDDES, as Minister of Transport, will be to correct the grave injustice by which a fragile spinster of seven stone weight is charged at the same rate as a bloated profiteer of seventeen stone; and that an ukase will be issued requiring all passengers to pay by weight at a uniform charge of one penny per pound for every hundred miles. Our artist has here depicted some of the far-reaching consequences of this drastic reform.]

FATHER, WHO CARRIES A CONSIDERABLE QUANTITY OF ADIPOSE DEPOSIT, HAS TO STAY AT HOME DURING THE SUMMER HOLIDAYS, AS IT COSTS TOO MUCH TO TAKE HIM WITH THE FAMILY.

WHEN PROCEEDING ON A JOURNEY DURING THE HEIGHT OF WINTER AUNTS SUSANNAH AND SERAPHINA WEAR THE VERY FLIMSIEST SUMMER CLOTHING SO AS TO REDUCE THE COST OF TRAVELLING.

STUDY OF A WELTER-WEIGHT EARNESTLY ENDEAVOURING TO QUALIFY FOR COMMERCIAL TRAVEL.

DAWN OF THE ERA OF THE FEATHER-WEIGHT COMMERCIAL TRAVELLER.

Vicar. "WHAT A FINE BIG BOY TOMMY IS GROWING!"
Proud Mother. "YES, SIR, HE'S ALREADY TWO-AND-THREE-HALFPENCE TO BRIGHTON."

BEFORE AND AFTER.
MR. ROBINSON DEFEATS THE MANAGEMENT.

HAVING TAKEN A RETURN-TICKET TO THE COUNTRY, WHERE HE HAS PUT ON FOUR STONE, HE SAVES THE EXTRA FIVE-AND-TENPENCE WHICH HE WOULD HAVE HAD TO PAY FOR THE HOMEWARD TRANSIT IF HE HAD TAKEN A SINGLE.

From *Punch*, 1919. Collection of Ken and Kate Baynes.
Photographer Gerald Pates

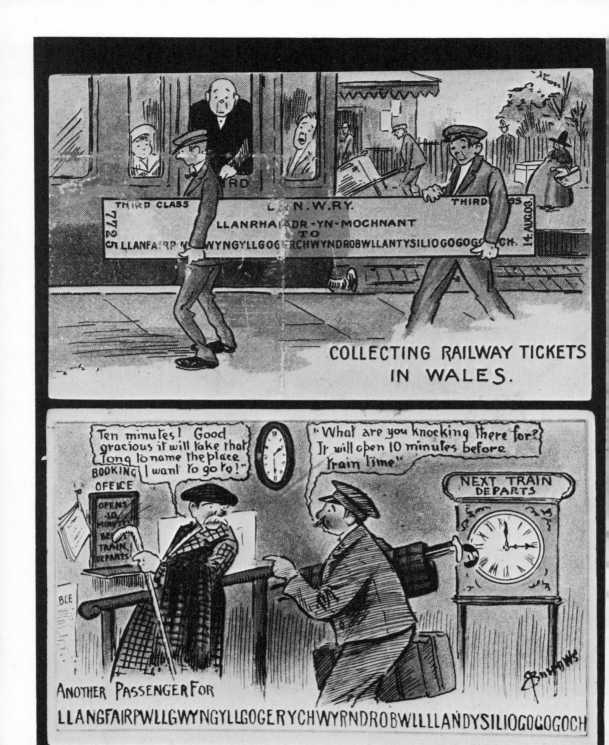

Two postcards from the collection of Peter Lawrence,
photographed by Chris Ridley

MORE REAL
THAN REALITY

railway fantasies

'The Constable on the Great Western Railway, who was
run over by the train, whilst taking his Tea'. G W R
Museum, Swindon. Photographers Cavill and Davison

Remarkably prophetic drawings by J. S. Jenkins from the
G W R Centenary number of the *Great Western Railway
Magazine*, 1935. G W R Museum, Swindon

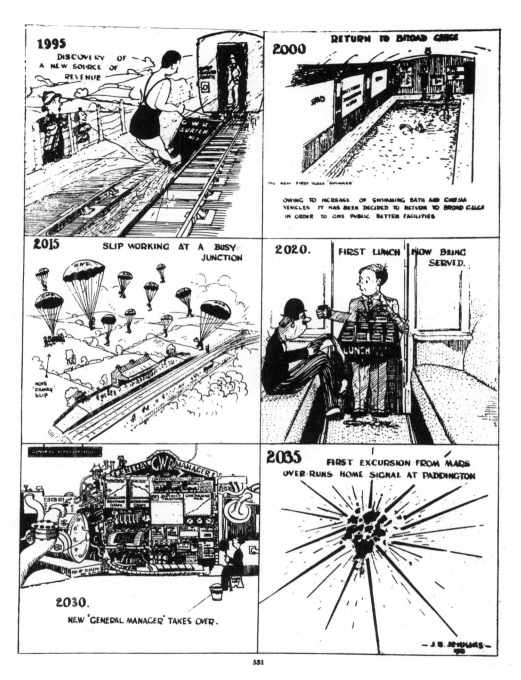

Endpapers from *The Wonder Book of Railways*. Ward Lock and Co Ltd
Collection of Ken and Kate Baynes. Photographer Gerald Pates

Endpapers from *The Wonder Book of Railways*. Ward Lock and Co Ltd
Collection of Ken and Kate Baynes. Photographer Gerald Pates

A WELL THOUGHT OUT AND NEARLY SUCCESSFUL
EXPERIMENT BY EARLY RAILWAY PIONEER

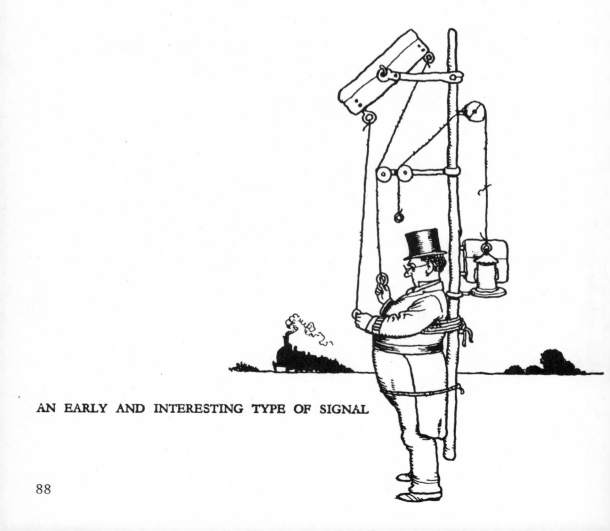

AN EARLY AND INTERESTING TYPE OF SIGNAL

EARLY METHODS OF ENGINE CLEANING

Three drawings by W Heath Robinson from *Railway
Ribaldry*, published by Gerald Duckworth & Co Ltd
Copyright Josephine Heath Robinson

TOO LATE ! A PATHETIC ATTEMPT TO ARREST THE PROGRESS OF THE RECORD BREAKING PLYMOUTH-LONDON TRAIN, MAY 9TH, 1904

THE FIRST DOG'S TICKET

Three drawings by W Heath Robinson from *Railway Ribaldry,* published by Gerald Duckworth & Co Ltd, Copyright Josephine Heath Robinson

THE BUILDING OF SALTASH BRIDGE

A Scene on the Political Rail Road, cartoon dating from
1841. Only eleven years after the opening of the
Liverpool and Manchester, railways were already familiar
enough to provide a fantasy setting for political jokes.
National Railway Museum, York

From *Punch,* 1866. Mr. Punch has a dream. It is a
fantasy in which all the problems of London are resolved.
Along with the intransigence of gas companies, the
intolerable traffic jams and the insolence of public
servants, railways take their share of criticism. 'I forbade
engines to scream in or within five miles of the Metropolis,
and I took away all their powers of building bridges over
the streets until they had invented some way of running
trains on them without any noise.' Collection of Ken and
Kate Baynes. Photographer Gerald Pates

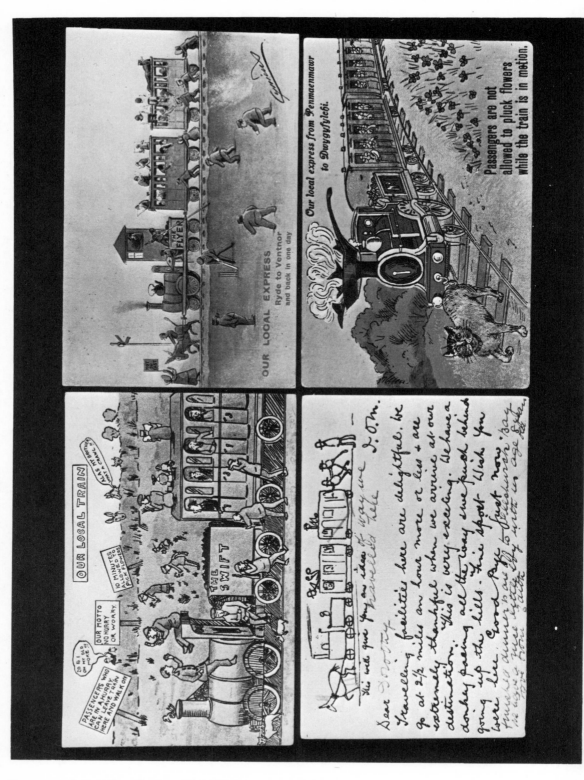

Four postcards from the collection of Peter Lawrence,
photographed by Chris Ridley

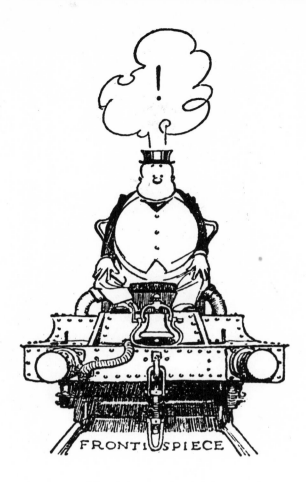

FRONTISPIECE

Frontispiece from *The Pop Annual* published by The
Daily Graphic and Sunday Graphic Ltd. Collection of
Ken and Kate Baynes

From *Punch's* Almanack for 1846. Mansell Collection,
London. Photographed by Gerald Pates

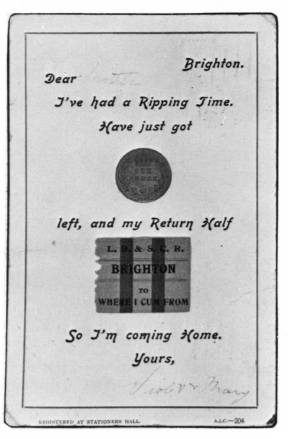

Brighton.

Dear ~~Mother~~

I've had a Ripping Time.

Have just got

left, and my Return Half

L. B. & S. C. R.

BRIGHTON

TO

WHERE I CUM FROM

So I'm coming Home.

Yours,

~~Violet & Mary~~

THE END

I'm catching the last train home

Two postcards from the collection of Peter Lawrence,
photographed by Chris Ridley